POEMS TO SINK YOUR TEETH INTO

More poetry available from
Macmillan Collector's Library

My Gothic Heart ed. Charlie Castelletti

Poems of Childhood introduced by Michael Morpurgo

Poems for Travellers introduced by Paul Theroux

Poems on Nature introduced by Helen Macdonald

Poems for Christmas introduced by Judith Flanders

Poems for Love introduced by Joanna Trollope

Leaves of Grass: Selected Poems by Walt Whitman

Selected Poems by John Keats

The Golden Treasury ed. Francis Turner Palgrave

Poetry of the First World War ed. Marcus Clapham

A Shropshire Lad by A. E. Housman

The Rime of the Ancient Mariner by Samuel Taylor Coleridge

Poems of Thomas Hardy by Thomas Hardy

Tales and Poems by Edgar Allan Poe

Selected Verse by Rudyard Kipling

The Sonnets by William Shakespeare

Collected Poems by W. B. Yeats

Poems to Swipe Right To ed. Charlie Castelletti

A Golden Treasury of Irish Verse ed. Lennox Robinson

Leaves of Grass: Selected Poems by Walt Whitman

Selected Poems by John Keats

Collected Poems by W. B. Yeats

The Sonnets by William Shakespeare

Poetry of the First World War ed. Marcus Clapham

Tales and Poems by Edgar Allan Poe

The Rime of the Ancient Mariner by Samuel Taylor Coleridge

POEMS TO SINK YOUR TEETH INTO

Edited and introduced by
CHARLIE CASTELLETTI

MACMILLAN COLLECTOR'S LIBRARY

This collection first published 2026 by Macmillan Collector's Library
an imprint of Pan Macmillan
The Smithson, 6 Briset Street, London EC1M 5NR
EU representative: Macmillan Publishers Ireland Ltd, 1st Floor,
The Liffey Trust Centre, 117–126 Sheriff Street Upper,
Dublin 1, D01 YC43
Associated companies throughout the world

ISBN 978-1-0350-6422-9

1 3 5 7 9 8 6 4 2

A CIP catalogue record for this book is available from the British Library.

Cover and endpaper design: Tiana-Jane Dunlop, Pan Macmillan Art Department
Typeset in Plantin by Six Red Marbles UK, Thetford, Norfolk
Printed and bound in China by Imago

Contents

GHOSTS & HAUNTINGS

SIRENS & SEA CREATURES

WITCHES & SPELLS

FAIRIES & GOBLINS

DRAGONS & MONSTERS

MOON & STARS

Introduction

CHARLIE CASTELLETTI

Vampires, angels, fae, demons, witches . . . magical and supernatural beings are more popular than ever. What is it that makes these creatures so appealing to us? Why are they back with such strength? How have they been portrayed throughout the ages, and what might those depictions say about us?

Shakespeare writes of powerful magic and the reawakening of the dead in his play *The Tempest*. The protagonist, Prospero, can rouse the dead, saying: 'graves at my command / Have waked their sleepers, oped, and let 'em forth / By my so potent art.' The supernatural beings featured in this anthology go beyond mythology, literature, ritual and storytelling; they are a 'potent' part of our lives, present in all kinds of media and entertainment. They exist in novels, poems, films, dreams, even aesthetics and 'vibes', evoking macabre or spooky feelings, fear, curiosity and even longing.

Here you can expect to find the poetry of Lord Byron, Charles Baudelaire, John Milton, Christina Rossetti, Emily Dickinson, Edgar Allan Poe, Emily Brontë, Walt Whitman and so many more who have been moved, fascinated or enraptured by these beings for centuries, often using them as an allegory or a motif through which to comment on different aspects of their lives.

Poems to Sink Your Teeth Into takes you through eight themed sections. The first, 'Vampires and Seduction', explores a macabre obsession with love and lust through the figure of the vampire. The second, 'Angels and Demons', is concerned with the sacred, the demonic and the intersection between the two. Are they a mere figment of our imagination, a response to our prayers or sins? Or do they exist as a force for good? The third section, 'Ghosts and Hauntings', shows the supernatural leaching into our everyday lives. Are these spirits really here, confined to another plane? Why do we carry with us those who have come before?

The poems in section four take us leagues under the sea, where 'Sirens and Sea Creatures' lure men and women to their deaths with their beauty and their songs. A siren might be the perfect woman: an unattainable and therefore deadly construct. 'Witches and Spells' is our fifth section, moving from early modern extracts from Shakespeare and Milton all the way up to contemporary poetry by Nikita Gill, tracking what the symbol of the witch has meant throughout history. Is to be a witch to be a woman? Or is to be a woman to be a witch? Section six, 'Fairies and Goblins', takes us through faerie rings, enchanted gardens, goblin markets and more, while the seventh section, 'Dragons and Monsters', features everything weird and wonderful, from vengeful Furies to Lewis Carroll's Jabberwocky, kelpies and the Minotaur. Lastly, we end with a section on the 'Moon and Stars'. As well as being the focus for our eighth section, the celestial permeates this entire anthology, be it via moon magic, stardust, vampiric night or a witch bathing in the moonglow.

Most importantly, we only need to look inside these pages, or look around us, to see that magic, beauty and all things spooky and supernatural are never far away. So go forth and take a bite from each section; savour and relish the contents within. Whether you're in your spooky season or witchy era – or merely sipping a pumpkin spiced latte – there is much to learn from the beings who lurk in the shadows of our everyday . . .

POEMS TO SINK YOUR TEETH INTO

Vampires & Seduction

Oil and Blood

In tombs of gold and lapis lazuli
Bodies of holy men and women exude
Miraculous oil, odour of violet.

But under heavy loads of trampled clay
Lie bodies of the vampires full of blood;
Their shrouds are bloody and their lips are wet.

W. B. Yeats

from The Vampire Bride

And his faithful bride lay awake by his side,
'Till St Peter's clock toll'd one;
When a slumber deep o'er her senses did creep,
For the Demon's power had begun.

The taper's light was extinguish'd quite,
And the choristers all dropp'd to rest,
And the priest sunk down, like a monument stone,
With the cross on his bosom prest.

And again a bitter cry broke forth in agony,—
"Save me! for mercy! save!"
For Albert did hold the Spectre damp and cold,
And the couch smell'd like a grave!

"I am come—I am come! once again from the tomb,
In return for the ring which you gave;
That I am thine, and that thou art mine,
This nuptial pledge receive."

He lay like a corse 'neath the Demon's force,
And she wrapp'd him in a shroud;
And she fixed her teeth his heart beneath,
And she drank of the warm life-blood!

And ever and anon murmur'd the lips of stone,
"Soft and warm is this couch of thine,
Thou'lt to-morrow be laid on a colder bed—
Albert! that bed will be mine!"

Another bitter cry, and he senseless did lie,
For the fiend sucked his stifled breath;
And the blood flowed fast from his wounded breast,
And he suffered the pangs of death.

The morning light hath chased the night,
And the fiend hath its grasp withdrawn;
Away it flew, as the first cock crew
In sign of the blushing dawn.

Henry Thomas Liddell

from The Vampyre

"Young Sigismund, my once dear friend,
But now my persecutor foul,
Doth his malevolence extend
E'en to the torture of my soul.

"By night, when, wrapt in soundest sleep,
All mortals share a soft repose,
My soul doth dreadful vigils keep,
More keen than which hell scarcely
knows.

"From the drear mansions of the tomb,
From the low regions of the dead,
The ghost of Sigismund doth roam,
And dreadful haunts me in my bed!

"There, vested in infernal guise,
(By means to me not understood)
Close to my side the goblin lies,
And drinks away my vital blood!

"Sucks from my veins the streaming life,
  And drains the fountain of any heart!
O Gertrude, Gertrude! dearest wife!
  Unutterable is my smart.

"When surfeited, the goblin dire,
  With banqueting by suckled gore,
Will to his sepulchre retire,
  Till night invites him forth once more.

"Then will he dreadfully return,
  And from my veins life's juices drain;
Whilst, slumb'ring, I with anguish mourn,
  And toss with agonizing pain!

"Already I'm exhausted, spent;
  His carnival is nearly o'er,
My soul with agony is rent,
  To-morrow I shall be no more!

John Stagg

La Belle Dame sans Merci

A Ballad

I

O what can ail thee, knight-at-arms,
  Alone and palely loitering?
The sedge has withered from the lake,
  And no birds sing.

II

O what can ail thee, knight-at-arms,
  So haggard and so woe-begone?
The squirrel's granary is full,
  And the harvest's done.

III

I see a lily on thy brow,
  With anguish moist and fever-dew,
And on thy cheeks a fading rose
  Fast withereth too.

IV

I met a lady in the meads,
  Full beautiful – a faery's child,
Her hair was long, her foot was light,
  And her eyes were wild.

V

I made a garland for her head,
  And bracelets too, and fragrant zone;
She looked at me as she did love,
  And made sweet moan.

VI

I set her on my pacing steed,
  And nothing else saw all day long,
For sidelong would she bend, and sing
  A faery's song.

VII

She found me roots of relish sweet,
  And honey wild, and manna-dew,
And sure in language strange she said –
  'I love thee true'.

VIII

She took me to her elfin grot,
  And there she wept and sighed full sore,
And there I shut her wild wild eyes
  With kisses four.

IX

And there she lullèd me asleep
  And there I dreamed – Ah! woe betide! –
The latest dream I ever dreamt
  On the cold hill side.

X

I saw pale kings and princes too,
  Pale warriors, death-pale were they all;
They cried – 'La Belle Dame sans Merci
  Thee hath in thrall!'

XI

I saw their starved lips in the gloam,
  With horrid warning gapèd wide,
And I awoke and found me here,
  On the cold hill's side.

XII

And this is why I sojourn here
  Alone and palely loitering,
Though the sedge is withered from the lake,
  And no birds sing.

John Keats

The Vampire

A lily in a twilight place?
A moonflow'r in the lonely night?—
Strange beauty of a woman's face
  Of wildflow'r-white!

The rain that hangs a star's green ray
Slim on a leaf-point's restlessness,
Is not so glimmering green and gray
  As was her dress.

I drew her dark hair from her eyes,
And in their deeps beheld a while
Such shadowy moonlight as the skies
  Of Hell may smile.

She held her mouth up redly wan,
And burning cold,—I bent and kissed
Such rosy snow as some wild dawn
  Makes of a mist.

God shall not take from me that hour,
When round my neck her white arms clung!
When 'neath my lips, like some fierce flower,
  Her white throat swung!

Or words she murmured while she leaned!
Witch-words, she holds me softly by,—
The spell that binds me to a fiend
  Until I die.

Madison Julius Cawein

from Christabel

PART I

Beneath the lamp the lady bowed,
And slowly rolled her eyes around;
Then drawing in her breath aloud
Like one that shuddered, she unbound
The cincture from beneath her breast:
Her silken robe, and inner vest,
Dropt to her feet, and full in view,
Behold! her bosom and half her side—

A sight to dream of, not to tell!
O shield her! shield sweet Christabel!
Yet Geraldine nor speaks nor stirs;
Ah! what a stricken look was hers!

Deep from within she seems half-way
To lift some weight with sick assay,
And eyes the maid and seeks delay;
Then suddenly, as one defied,
Collects herself in scorn and pride,
And lay down by the Maiden's side!—
And in her arms the maid she took,

Ah well-a-day!
And with low voice and doleful look
These words did say:
In the touch of this bosom there worketh a spell,
Which is lord of thy utterance, Christabel!
Thou knowest to-night, and wilt know
to-morrow,
This mark of my shame, this seal of my sorrow;
But vainly thou warrest,
For this is alone in
Thy power to declare,
That in the dim forest
Thou heard'st a low moaning,
And found'st a bright lady, surpassingly fair;
And didst bring her home with thee in love and
in charity,
To shield her and shelter her from the
damp air.

PART II

The air is still! through mist and cloud
That merry peal comes ringing loud;
And Geraldine shakes off her dread,
And rises lightly from the bed;
Puts on her silken vestments white,

And tricks her hair in lovely plight,
And nothing doubting of her spell
Awakens the lady Christabel.
"Sleep you, sweet lady Christabel?
I trust that you have rested well."
And Christabel awoke and spied
The same who lay down by her side—
O rather say, the same whom she
Raised up beneath the old oak tree!
Nay, fairer yet! and yet more fair!
For she, belike, hath drunken deep
Of all the blessedness of sleep!
And while she spake, her looks, her air
Such gentle thankfulness declare,
That (so it seemed) her girded vests
Grew tight beneath her heaving breasts.
"Sure I have sinn'd!" said Christabel,
"Now heaven be praised if all be well!"
And in low faltering tones, yet sweet,
Did she the lofty lady greet,
With such perplexity of mind
As dreams too lively leave behind.

Samuel Taylor Coleridge

The Vampire's Metamorphoses

The woman meanwhile, twisting like a snake
On hot coals and kneading her breasts against the steel
Of her corset, from her mouth red as strawberries
Let flow these words impregnated with musk:
—"I, I have moist lips, and I know the art
Of losing old Conscience in the depths of a bed.
I dry all tears on my triumphant breasts
And make old men laugh with the laughter of children.
I replace, for him who sees me nude, without veils,
The moon, the sun, the stars and the heavens!
I am, my dear scholar, so learned in pleasure
That when I smother a man in my fearful arms,
Or when, timid and licentious, frail and robust,
I yield my bosom to biting kisses
On those two soft cushions which swoon with emotion,
The powerless angels would damn themselves for me!"

When she had sucked out all the marrow from
my bones
And I languidly turned toward her
To give back an amorous kiss, I saw no more
Than a wine-skin with gluey sides, all full
of pus!
Frozen with terror, I closed both my eyes,
And when I opened them to the bright light,
At my side, instead of the robust manikin
Who seemed to have laid in a store of blood,
There quivered confusedly a heap of old bones,
Which of themselves gave forth the cry of a
weather-cock
Or of a sign on the end of an iron rod
That the wind swings to and fro on a winter
night.

Charles Baudelaire

from The Giaour

And fire unquench'd, unquenchable,
Around, within, thy heart shall dwell;
Nor ear can hear nor tongue can tell
The tortures of that inward hell!
But first, on earth as Vampire sent,
Thy corse shall from its tomb be rent:
Then ghastly haunt thy native place,
And suck the blood of all thy race;
There from thy daughter, sister, wife,
At midnight drain the stream of life;
Yet loathe the banquet which perforce
Must feed thy livid living corse:
Thy victims ere they yet expire
Shall know the dæmon for their sire,
As cursing thee, thou cursing them,
Thy flowers are wither'd on the stem.
But one that for thy crime must fall,
The youngest, most beloved of all,
Shall bless thee with a *father's* name—
That word shall wrap thy heart in flame!
Yet must thou end thy task, and mark
Her cheek's last tinge, her eye's last spark,
And the last glassy glance must view

Which freezes o'er its lifeless blue;
Then with unhallow'd hand shalt tear
The tresses of her yellow hair,
Of which in life a lock when shorn
Affection's fondest pledge was worn;
But now is borne away by thee,
Memorial of thine agony!

Lord Byron

The Vampire

My dear young maiden clingeth
unbending, fast and firm
To all the long-held teaching
Of a mother ever true;
As in vampires unmortal
Folk on the Theyse's portal
Heyduck-like do believe.
But my Christine thou dost
  dally,
And wilt my loving parry
Till I myself avenging
To a vampire's health a-drinking
Him toast in pale tockay.

And as softly thou art sleeping
To thee shall I come creeping
And thy life's blood drain away.
And so shalt thou be trembling
For thus shall I be kissing
And death's threshold thou'
  it crossing
With fear, in my cold arms.
And last shall I thee question

Compared to such instruction
What are a mother's charms?

Heinrich August Ossenfelder

Angels & Demons

The Angel

I dreamt a dream! What can it mean?
And that I was a maiden Queen
Guarded by an Angel mild:
Witless woe was ne'er beguiled!

And I wept both night and day,
And he wiped my tears away;
And I wept both day and night,
And hid from him my heart's delight.

So he took his wings, and fled;
Then the morn blushed rosy red.
I dried my tears, and armed my fears
With ten thousand shields and spears.

Soon my Angel came again;
I was armed, he came in vain;
For the time of youth was fled,
And grey hairs were on my head.

William Blake

The Two Angels

Two angels, one of Life and one of Death,
    Passed o'er our village as the morning broke;
The dawn was on their faces, and beneath,
    The sombre houses hearsed with plumes of
        smoke.

Their attitude and aspect were the same,
    Alike their features and their robes of white;
But one was crowned with amaranth, as with
  flame,
    And one with asphodels, like flakes of light.

I saw them pause on their celestial way;
    Then said I, with deep fear and doubt
        oppressed,
"Beat not so loud, my heart, lest thou betray
    The place where thy beloved are at rest!"

And he who wore the crown of asphodels,
    Descending, at my door began to knock,
And my soul sank within me, as in wells
    The waters sink before an earthquake's
        shock.

I recognized the nameless agony,
The terror and the tremor and the pain,
That oft before had filled or haunted me,
And now returned with threefold strength again.

The door I opened to my heavenly guest,
And listened, for I thought I heard God's voice;
And, knowing whatsoe'er he sent was best,
Dared neither to lament nor to rejoice.

Then with a smile, that filled the house with light,
"My errand is not Death, but Life," he said;
And ere I answered, passing out of sight,
On his celestial embassy he sped.

'T was at thy door, O friend! and not at mine,
The angel with the amaranthine wreath,
Pausing, descended, and with voice divine,
Whispered a word that had a sound like Death.

Then fell upon the house a sudden gloom,
A shadow on those features fair and thin;
And softly, from that hushed and darkened room,
Two angels issued, where but one went in.

All is of God! If he but wave his hand,
The mists collect, the rain falls thick and loud,
Till, with a smile of light on sea and land,
Lo! he looks back from the departing cloud.

Angels of Life and Death alike are his;
Without his leave they pass no threshold o'er;
Who, then, would wish or dare, believing this,
Against his messengers to shut the door?

Henry Wadsworth Longfellow

The Daemon Lover

'O where have you been, my long, long love,
This long seven years and mair?'
'O I'm come to seek my former vows
Ye granted me before.'

'O hold your tongue of your former vows,
For they will breed sad strife;
O hold your tongue of your former vows,
For I am become a wife.'

He turned him right and round about,
And the tear blinded his ee:
'I wad never hae trodden on Irish ground,
If it had not been for thee.

'I might hae had a king's daughter,
Far, far beyond the sea;
I might have had a king's daughter,
Had it not been for love o thee.'

'If ye might have had a king's daughter,
Yer sel ye had to blame;
Ye might have taken the king's daughter,
For ye kend that I was nane.

'If I was to leave my husband dear,
And my two babes also,
O what have you to take me to,
If with you I should go?'

'I hae seven ships upon the sea—
The eighth brought me to land—
With four-and-twenty bold mariners,
And music on every hand.'

She has taken up her two little babes,
Kissd them baith cheek and chin:
'O fair ye weel, my ain two babes,
For I'll never see you again.'

She set her foot upon the ship,
No mariners could she behold;
But the sails were o the taffetie,
And the masts o the beaten gold.

She had not sailed a league, a league,
A league but barely three,
When dismal grew his countenance,
And drumlie grew his ee.

They had not saild a league, a league,
A league but barely three,
Until she espied his cloven foot,
And she wept right bitterlie.

'O hold your tongue of your weeping,' says he,
'Of your weeping now let me be;
I will shew you how the lilies grow
On the banks of Italy.'

'O what hills are yon, yon pleasant hills,
That the sun shines sweetly on?'
'O yon are the hills of heaven,' he said,
'Where you will never win.'

'O whaten a mountain is yon,' she said,
'All so dreary wi frost and snow?'
'O yon is the mountain of hell,' he cried,
'Where you and I will go.'

He strack the tap-mast wi his hand,
  The fore-mast wi his knee,
And he brake that gallant ship in twain,
  And sank her in the sea.

Anon.

The Devil's Thoughts

I.

From his brimstone bed at break of day
A walking the Devil is gone,
To visit his snug little farm the Earth,
And see how his stock goes on.

II.

Over the hill and over the dale,
And he went over the plain,
And backward and forward he switched his long tail
As a gentleman switches his cane.

III.

And how then was the Devil drest?
Oh! he was in his Sunday's best:
His jacket was red and his breeches were blue,
And there was a hole where the tail came through.

IV.

He saw a Lawyer killing a viper
On a dunghill hard by his own stable;
And the Devil smiled, for it put him in mind
Of Cain and his brother Abel.

V.

He saw an Apothecary on a white horse
Ride by on his vocations;
And the Devil thought of his old friend
Death in the Revelations.

VI.

He saw a cottage with a double coach-house,
A cottage of gentility;
And the Devil did grin, for his darling sin
Is pride that apes humility.

VII.

He peeped into a rich bookseller's shop,
Quoth he, "We are both of one college!
For I sate myself, like a cormorant, once
Hard by the tree of knowledge."

VIII.

Down the river did glide, with wind and with
  tide,
    A pig with vast celerity;
And the Devil look'd wise as he saw how the
  while,
It cut its own throat. "There!" quoth he with a
  smile,
    "Goes England's commercial prosperity."

IX.

As he went through Cold-Bath Fields he saw
    A solitary cell;
And the Devil was pleased, for it gave him a hint
    For improving his prisons in Hell.

X.

He saw a Turnkey in a trice
    Fetter a troublesome blade;
"Nimbly," quoth he, "do the fingers move
    If a man be but used to his trade."

XI.

He saw the same Turnkey unfetter a man
  With but little expedition,
Which put him in mind of the long debate
  On the Slave-trade abolition.

XII.

He saw an old acquaintance
  As he passed by a Methodist meeting;—
She holds a consecrated key,
  And the Devil nods her a greeting.

XIII.

She turned up her nose, and said,
  "Avaunt! my name's Religion,"
And she looked to Mr.——
  And leered like a love-sick pigeon.

XIV.

He saw a certain minister
  (A minister to his mind)
Go up into a certain House,
  With a majority behind.

XV.

The Devil quoted Genesis,
  Like a very learned clerk,
How "Noah and his creeping things
  Went up into the Ark."

XVI.

He took from the poor,
  And he gave to the rich,
And he shook hands with a Scotchman,
  For he was not afraid of the——

XVII.

General ——— burning face
  He saw with consternation,
And back to hell his way did he take,
For the Devil thought by a slight mistake
  It was general conflagration.

Samuel Taylor Coleridge

Lucifer in Starlight

On a starred night Prince Lucifer uprose.
Tired of his dark dominion swung the fiend
Above the rolling ball in cloud part screened,
Where sinners hugged their spectre of repose.
Poor prey to his hot fit of pride were those.
And now upon his western wing he leaned,
Now his huge bulk o'er Afric's sands careened,
Now the black planet shadowed Arctic snows.
Soaring through wider zones that pricked his scars
With memory of the old revolt from Awe,
He reached a middle height, and at the stars,
Which are the brain of heaven, he looked, and sank
Around the ancient track marched rank on rank,
The army of unalterable law.

George Meredith

from Paradise Lost

Th' infernal Serpent; he it was, whose guile
Stir'd up with envy and Revenge, deceiv'd
The Mother of Mankind, what time his Pride
Had cast him out from Heav'n, with all
  his Host
Of Rebel Angels, by whose aid aspiring
To set himself in Glory above his Peers,
He trusted to have equall'd the Most High,
If he oppos'd; and with ambitious aim
Against the Throne and Monarchy of God
Rais'd impious War in Heav'n and Battel proud
With vain attempt. Him the Almighty Power
Hurl'd headlong flaming from th' Ethereal Sky
With hideous ruine and combustion down
To bottomless perdition, there to dwell
In Adamantine Chains and penal Fire,
Who durst defie th' Omnipotent to Arms.

John Milton

An Angel in the House

How sweet it were, if without feeble fright,
Or dying of the dreadful beauteous sight,
An angel came to us, and we could bear
To see him issue from the silent air
At evening in our room, and bend on ours
His divine eyes, and bring us from his bowers
News of dear friends, and children who have
never
Been dead indeed,—as we shall know for ever.
Alas! we think not what we daily see
About our hearths,—angels, that *are* to be,
Or may be if they will, and we prepare
Their souls and ours to meet in happy air,—
A child, a friend, a wife whose soft heart sings
In unison with ours, breeding its future wings.

James Henry Leigh Hunt

Angel or Demon

You call me an angel of love and of light,
A being of goodness and heavenly fire,
Sent out from God's kingdom to guide you aright,
In paths where your spirit may mount and aspire.
You say that I glow like a star on its course,
Like a ray from the altar, a spark from the source.

Now list to my answer; let all the world hear it,
I speak unafraid what I know to be true:—
A pure, faithful love is the creative spirit
Which makes women angels! I live but in you.
We are bound soul to soul by life's holiest laws;
If I am an Angel—why, you are the cause.

As my ship skims the sea, I look up from the deck,
Fair, firm at the wheel shines Love's beautiful form,

And shall I curse the barque that last night
went to wreck,
By the Pilot abandoned to darkness and
storm?
My craft is no stauncher, she too had been
lost—
Had the wheelman deserted, or slept at his post.

I laid down the wealth of my soul at your feet
(Some woman does this for some man
every day).
No desperate creature who walks in the street
Has a wickeder heart than I might have,
I say,
Had you wantonly misused the treasures
you won,
As so many men with heart riches have
done.

This fire from God's altar, this holy love-flame
That burns like sweet incense for ever
for you,
Might now be a wild conflagration of shame,
Had you tortured my heart, or been base or
untrue.

For angels and devils are cast in one mould,
Till love guides them upward, or downward, I hold.

I tell you the women who make fervent wives
And sweet tender mothers, had Fate been less fair,
Are the women who might have abandoned their lives
To the madness that springs from and ends in despair.
As the fire on the hearth which sheds brightness around,
Neglected, may level the walls to the ground.

The world makes grave errors in judging these things:
Great good and great evil are born in one breast.
Love horns us and hoofs us—or gives us our wings,
And the best could be worst, as the worst could be best.

You must thank your own worth for what I grew
  to be,
    For the demon lurked under the angel
      in me.

Ella Wheeler Wilcox

Ghosts & Hauntings

Strange Meeting

It seemed that out of battle I escaped
Down some profound dull tunnel, long since
  scooped
Through granites which titanic wars had
  groined.
Yet also there encumbered sleepers groaned,
Too fast in thought or death to be bestirred.
Then, as I probed them, one sprang up, and
  stared
With piteous recognition in fixed eyes,
Lifting distressful hands as if to bless.
And by his smile, I knew that sullen hall,
By his dead smile I knew we stood in Hell.
With a thousand pains that vision's face was
  grained;
Yet no blood reached there from the upper
  ground,
And no guns thumped, or down the flues made
  moan.
"Strange friend," I said, "here is no cause to
  mourn."
"None," said the other, "save the undone years,
The hopelessness. Whatever hope is yours,

Was my life also; I went hunting wild
After the wildest beauty in the world,
Which lies not calm in eyes, or braided hair,
But mocks the steady running of the hour,
And if it grieves, grieves richlier than here.
For by my glee might many men have laughed,
And of my weeping something had been left,
Which must die now. I mean the truth untold,
The pity of war, the pity war distilled.
Now men will go content with what we spoiled.
Or, discontent, boil bloody, and be spilled.
They will be swift with swiftness of the tigress,
None will break ranks, though nations trek
  from progress.
Courage was mine, and I had mystery,
Wisdom was mine, and I had mastery;
To miss the march of this retreating world
Into vain citadels that are not walled.
Then, when much blood had clogged their
  chariot-wheels
I would go up and wash them from sweet wells,
Even with truths that lie too deep for taint.
I would have poured my spirit without stint
But not through wounds; not on the cess
  of war.

Foreheads of men have bled where no wounds
  were.
I am the enemy you killed, my friend.
I knew you in this dark; for so you frowned
Yesterday through me as you jabbed and killed.
I parried; but my hands were loath and cold.
Let us sleep now . . ."

Wilfred Owen

Shadwell Stair

I am the ghost of Shadwell Stair.
 Along the wharves by the water-house,
 And through the dripping slaughter-house,
I am the shadow that walks there.

Yet I have flesh both firm and cool,
 And eyes tumultuous as the gems
 Of moons and lamps in the lapping Thames
When dusk sails wavering down the pool.

Shuddering the purple street-arc burns
 Where I watch always; from the banks
 Dolorously the shipping clanks,
And after me a strange tide turns.

I walk till the stars of London wane
 And dawn creeps up the Shadwell Stair.
 But when the crowing syrens blare
I with another ghost am lain.

Wilfred Owen

The Poor Ghost

'Oh whence do you come, my dear friend, to me,
With your golden hair all fallen below your knee,
And your face as white as snowdrops on the lea,
And your voice as hollow as the hollow sea?'

'From the other world I come back to you:
My locks are uncurled with dripping drenching dew,
You know the old, whilst I know the new:
But to-morrow you shall know this too.'

'Oh not to-morrow into the dark, I pray;
Oh not to-morrow, too soon to go away:
Here I feel warm and well-content and gay:
Give me another year, another day.'

'Am I so changed in a day and a night
That mine own only love shrinks from me with fright,

Is fain to turn away to left or right
And cover up his eyes from the sight?'

'Indeed I loved you, my chosen friend,
I loved you for life, but life has an end;
Through sickness I was ready to tend:
But death mars all, which we cannot mend.

'Indeed I loved you; I love you yet,
If you will stay where your bed is set,
Where I have planted a violet,
Which the wind waves, which the dew
  makes wet.'

'Life is gone, then love too is gone,
It was a reed that I leant upon:
Never doubt I will leave you alone
And not wake you rattling bone with bone.

'I go home alone to my bed,
Dug deep at the foot and deep at the head,
Roofed in with a load of lead,
Warm enough for the forgotten dead.

'But why did your tears soak through the clay,
And why did your sobs wake me where I lay?
I was away, far enough away:
Let me sleep now till the Judgment Day.'

Christina Rossetti

The Hour and the Ghost

O love, love, hold me fast,
He draws me away from thee;
I cannot stem the blast,
Nor the cold strong sea:
Far away a light shines
Beyond the hills and pines;
It is lit for me.

BRIDEGROOM:

I have thee close, my dear,
No terror can come near;
Only far off the northern light shines clear.

GHOST:

Come with me, fair and false,
To our home, come home.
It is my voice that calls:
Once thou wast not afraid
When I woo'd, and said,
'Come, our nest is newly made'—
Now cross the tossing foam.

BRIDE:

Hold me one moment longer!
He taunts me with the past,
His clutch is waxing stronger;
Hold me fast, hold me fast.
He draws me from thy heart,
And I cannot withhold:
He bids my spirit depart
With him into the cold:—
Oh bitter vows of old!

BRIDEGROOM:

Lean on me, hide thine eyes:
Only ourselves, earth and skies,
Are present here: be wise.

GHOST:

Lean on me, come away,
I will guide and steady:
Come, for I will not stay:
Come, for house and bed are ready.
Ah sure bed and house,

For better and worse, for life and death,
Goal won with shortened breath!
Come, crown our vows.

BRIDE:

One moment, one more word,
While my heart beats still,
While my breath is stirred
By my fainting will.
O friend, forsake me not,
Forget not as I forgot:
But keep thy heart for me,
Keep thy faith true and bright;
Through the lone cold winter night
Perhaps I may come to thee.

BRIDEGROOM:

Nay peace, my darling, peace:
Let these dreams and terrors cease:
Who spoke of death or change or aught but
ease?

GHOST:

O fair frail sin,
O poor harvest gathered in!
Thou shalt visit him again
To watch his heart grow cold:
To know the gnawing pain
I knew of old;
To see one much more fair
Fill up the vacant chair,
Fill his heart, his children bear;
While thou and I together,
In the outcast weather,
Toss and howl and spin.

Christina Rossetti

The Ghost

Softly as brown-eyed Angels rove
I will return to thy alcove,
And glide upon the night to thee,
Treading the shadows silently.

And I will give to thee, my own,
Kisses as icy as the moon,
And the caresses of a snake
Cold gliding in the thorny brake.

And when returns the livid morn
Thou shalt find all my place forlorn
And chilly, till the falling night.

Others would rule by tenderness
Over thy life and youthfulness,
But I would conquer thee by fright!

Charles Baudelaire

On His Deceased Wife

Methought I saw my late espousèd saint
    Brought to me like Alcestis from the grave,
    Whom Jove's great son to her glad husband gave,
    Rescued from death by force, though pale and faint.
Mine, as whom washed from spot of child-bed taint
    Purification in the old law did save;
    And such, as yet once more I trust to have
    Full sight of her in heav'n without restraint,
Came vested all in white, pure as her mind:
    Her face was veiled, yet to my fancied sight
    Love, sweetness, goodness, in her person shined
So clear, as in no face with more delight.
    But oh! as to embrace me she inclined,
    I waked, she fled, and day brought back my night.

John Milton

He Wishes His Beloved Were Dead

Were you but lying cold and dead,
And lights were paling out of the West,
You would come hither, and bend your head,
And I would lay my head on your breast;
And you would murmur tender words,
Forgiving me, because you were dead:
Nor would you rise and hasten away,
Though you have the will of the wild birds,
But know your hair was bound and wound
About the stars and moon and sun:
O would, beloved, that you lay
Under the dock-leaves in the ground,
While lights were paling one by one.

W. B. Yeats

My Spirit Will Not Haunt the Mound

My spirit will not haunt the mound
  Above my breast,
But travel, memory-possessed,
To where my tremulous being found
  Life largest, best.

My phantom-footed shape will go
  When nightfall grays
Hither and thither along the ways
I and another used to know
  In backward days.

And there you'll find me, if a jot
  You still should care
For me, and for my curious air;
If otherwise, then I shall not,
  For you, be there.

Thomas Hardy

The Apparition

When by thy scorne, O murdresse, I am dead,
And that thou thinkst thee free
From all solicitation from mee,
Then shall my ghost come to thy bed,
And thee, fain'd vestall, in worse armes
  shall see;
Then thy sicke taper will begin to winke,
And he, whose thou art then, being tyr'd before,
Will, if thou stirre, or pinch to wake him, thinke
    Thou call'st for more,
And in false sleepe will from thee shrinke,
And then poore Aspen wretch, neglected thou
Bath'd in a cold quicksilver sweat wilt lye
    A veryer ghost then I;
What I will say, I will not tell thee now,
Lest that preserve thee'; and since my love is
  spent,
I'had rather thou shouldst painfully repent,
Then by my threatnings rest still innocent.

John Donne

Haunted Houses

All houses wherein men have lived and died
Are haunted houses. Through the open doors
The harmless phantoms on their errands glide,
With feet that make no sound upon the floors.

We meet them at the door-way, on the stair,
Along the passages they come and go,
Impalpable impressions on the air,
A sense of something moving to and fro.

There are more guests at table, than the hosts
Invited; the illuminated hall
Is thronged with quiet, inoffensive ghosts,
As silent as the pictures on the wall.

The stranger at my fireside cannot see
The forms I see, nor hear the sounds I hear;
He but perceives what is; while unto me
All that has been is visible and clear.

We have no title-deeds to house or lands;
Owners and occupants of earlier dates
From graves forgotten stretch their dusty hands,
And hold in mortmain still their old estates.

The spirit-world around this world of sense
Floats like an atmosphere, and everywhere
Wafts through these earthly mists and vapors dense
A vital breath of more ethereal air.

Our little lives are kept in equipoise
By opposite attractions and desires;
The struggle of the instinct that enjoys,
And the more noble instinct that aspires.

These perturbations, this perpetual jar
Of earthly wants and aspirations high,
Come from the influence of an unseen star,
An undiscovered planet in our sky.

And as the moon from some dark gate of cloud
Throws o'er the sea a floating bridge of light,

Across whose trembling planks our fancies
crowd
Into the realm of mystery and night, —

So from the world of spirits there descends
A bridge of light, connecting it with this,
O'er whose unsteady floor, that sways and
bends,
Wander our thoughts above the dark abyss.

Henry Wadsworth Longfellow

One Need Not Be a Chamber – to be Haunted

One need not be a chamber to be haunted,
One need not be a house;
The brain has corridors surpassing
Material place,

Far safer, of a midnight meeting
External ghost,
Than an interior confronting
That whiter host.

Far safer through an Abbey gallop,
The stones achase,
Than, moonless, one's own self encounter
In lonesome place.

Ourself, behind ourself concealed,
Should startle most;
Assassin, hid in our apartment,
Be horror's least.

The prudent carries a revolver,
He bolts the door,
O'erlooking a superior spectre
More near.

Emily Dickinson

Sirens & Sea Creatures

Mermaid Becomes Merwife

Hands slashed by coral and rock,
flowering stems bleed on her palms.

Swaddled in silk to conceal her tail:
six woven yards of crimson brocade.

Wedding guests in scarlet or saffron –
blue or green risk summoning oceans.

A woman paints eyes on closed lids,
another plaits gold in sea tangle hair.

Wrists bound to his, mermaid feels
the sacred fire tongue at her throat.

Softly, a priest chants incantations.
He yanks her chain until she nods *yes*.

Gita Ralleigh

A Sea-Spell

Her lute hangs shadowed in the apple-tree,
While flashing fingers weave the sweet-
strung spell
Between its chords; and as the wild notes
swell,
The sea-bird for those branches leaves the sea.
But to what sound her listening ear stoops she?
What netherworld gulf-whispers doth
she hear,
In answering echoes from what planisphere,
Along the wind, along the estuary?

She sinks into her spell: and when full soon
Her lips move and she soars into her song,
What creatures of the midmost main shall
throng
In furrowed surf-clouds to the summoning rune:
Till he, the fated mariner, hears her cry,
And up her rock, bare-breasted, comes
to die?

Dante Gabriel Rossetti

The Siren

My voice is sweeter than the lute,
  My form is passing fair,
My lips are like the scarlet fruit
  The coral-branches bear.

My teeth are whiter than the pearls
  Men seek beneath the brine,
And when I shake my dripping curls
  Far brighter jewels shine.

My russet curls, whose golden tips
  Half hide a breast that swells
As pink and pearly as the lips
  That laugh on spike-back'd shells!

My eyes reflect the glimmer cast
  When seas lie calm and deep,
Where, under rotting spar and mast,
  The silent sailors sleep.

Oft have I dragged them from the sands,—
  They cannot make demur,—
And pulled the gold rings from their hands:
  They neither speak nor stir

So stark they lie! Yet one, alone,
  Awoke to find me fair
(This harp is made of his breast-bone,
  Its strings were once his hair):

A merry moon we pass'd, and more,
  And then upon him came
Some wanton memory of the shore,—
  He breathed a woman's name,

Wherefore I made him sleep again,
  So sound, he could not stir,
But first I suck'd his heart and brain,
  Lest he should dream of her.

Before he slept he spake strange words;
  These were the words he said:
"Your song is blither than the bird's,
  Your lips are ripe and red,

"Your breast is white, your eyes are blue,
  Yet you cannot understand
Or love your love as the maidens do
  That live upon the land!"

So, since, whene'er the sun is low
  And length'ning shadows fall,
And straying lovers come and go
  Along the grey sea-wall,

Amongst the rocks I crouch me down,
  To hear what they may say,
And learn this thing I have not known—
  To love the land-girls' way.

But oft I hear them moan and sigh,
  And often weep for woe;
The summer nights are going by,
  Yet this is all I know!

So mine must be the wiser way,
  For all my sweetheart said;
I made far merrier than they,
  The moon that I was wed.

And he was mine—my very own!
I clasped him firm and fair!
(This harp is made of his breast-bone,
Its strings were once his hair.)

Violet Fane

The Mermaid

I

Who would be
A mermaid fair,
Singing alone,
Combing her hair
Under the sea,
In a golden curl
With a comb of pearl,
On a throne?

II

I would be a mermaid fair;
I would sing to myself the whole of the day;
With a comb of pearl I would comb my hair;
And still as I comb'd I would sing and say,
'Who is it loves me? who loves not me?'
I would comb my hair till my ringlets would fall
Low adown, low adown,
From under my starry sea-bud crown
Low adown and around,
And I should look like a fountain of gold
Springing alone

With a shrill inner sound,
Over the throne
In the midst of the hall;
Till that great sea-snake under the sea
From his coiled sleeps in the central deeps
Would slowly trail himself sevenfold
Round the hall where I sate, and look in at
the gate
With his large calm eyes for the love of me.
And all the mermen under the sea
Would feel their immortality
Die in their hearts for the love of me.

III

But at night I would wander away, away,
I would fling on each side my low-flowing
locks,
And lightly vault from the throne and play
With the mermen in and out of the rocks;
We would run to and fro, and hide and seek,
On the broad sea-wolds in the crimson
shells,
Whose silvery spikes are nighest the sea.
But if any came near I would call and shriek,
And adown the steep like a wave I would leap

From the diamond-ledges that jut from the
dells;
For I would not be kiss'd by all who would list,
Of the bold merry mermen under the sea.
They would sue me, and woo me, and flatter me,
In the purple twilights under the sea;
But the king of them all would carry me,
Woo me, and win me, and marry me,
In the branching jaspers under the sea.
Then all the dry-pied things that be
In the hueless mosses under the sea
Would curl round my silver feet silently,
All looking up for the love of me.
And if I should carol aloud, from aloft
All things that are forked, and horned, and soft
Would lean out from the hollow sphere of
the sea,
All looking down for the love of me.

Alfred, Lord Tennyson

The Merman

I

Who would be
A merman bold,
Sitting alone,
Singing alone
Under the sea,
With a crown of gold,
On a throne?

II

    I would be a merman bold,
I would sit and sing the whole of the day;
I would fill the sea-halls with a voice of power;
But at night I would roam abroad and play
With the mermaids in and out of the rocks,
Dressing their hair with the white sea-flower;
And holding them back by their flowing locks
I would kiss them often under the sea,
And kiss them again till they kiss'd me
    Laughingly, laughingly;
And then we would wander away, away,
To the pale-green sea-groves straight and high,
    Chasing each other merrily.

III

There would be neither moon nor star;
But the wave would make music above us afar –
Low thunder and light in the magic night –
    Neither moon nor star.
We would call aloud in the dreamy dells,
Call to each other and whoop and cry
    All night, merrily, merrily.
They would pelt me with starry spangles and
  shells,
Laughing and clapping their hands between,
    All night, merrily, merrily,
But I would throw to them back in mine
Turkis and agate and almondine;
Then leaping out upon them unseen
I would kiss them often under the sea,
And kiss them again till they kiss'd me
    Laughingly, laughingly.
O, what a happy life were mine
Under the hollow-hung ocean green!
Soft are the moss-beds under the sea;
We would live merrily, merrily.

Alfred, Lord Tennyson

from A Man Young and Old

III

A mermaid found a swimming lad,
Picked him for her own,
Pressed her body to his body,
Laughed; and plunging down
Forgot in cruel happiness
That even lovers drown.

W. B. Yeats

The Mermaid Sat on the Carlin Stane

The mermaid sat on the Carlin stane,
A-kaimin her gowden hair,
The may ne'er was in Clydesdale wide
Was ever hauf sae fair.

Anon.

The Song of Wandering Aengus

I went out to the hazel wood,
Because a fire was in my head,
And cut and peeled a hazel wand,
And hooked a berry to a thread;
And when white moths were on the wing,
And moth-like stars were flickering out,
I dropped the berry in a stream
And caught a little silver trout.

When I had laid it on the floor
I went to blow the fire aflame,
But something rustled on the floor,
And some one called me by my name:
It had become a glimmering girl
With apple blossom in her hair
Who called me by my name and ran
And faded through the brightening air.

Though I am old with wandering
Through hollow lands and hilly lands,
I will find out where she has gone,
And kiss her lips and take her hands;
And walk among long dappled grass,

And pluck till time and times are done
The silver apples of the moon,
The golden apples of the sun.

W. B. Yeats

The Mermaid's Garden

Clare discovered this poem underneath her seaside spade.

Her garden far
Beneath the seas
Has shark-tooth fences,
Driftwood trees,
A coral bed of
Crimson flowers,
Seaweed hedges,
Three tall towers
(That once were masts
of ships, you know!),
A rocky bank
Where starfish glow,
A maze of blue anemones
(That tremble in
The salty breeze),
A marble statue
Old and grand
(She found it buried
In the sand),
A pathway made

From pearly shells
And plants that grow
In broken bells,
While stripy fish
With jewel eyes
Dart about like
Butterflies . . .

(And when you dream
Perhaps you'll creep
Around her garden
In your sleep.)

Clare Bevan

Witches & Spells

from Macbeth

ALL

Double, double toil and trouble;
Fire, burn; and, caldron, bubble.

SECOND WITCH

Fillet of a fenny snake,
In the caldron boil and bake;
Eye of newt, and toe of frog,
Wool of bat, and tongue of dog,
Adder's fork, and blind-worm's sting,
Lizard's leg, and howlet's wing,—
For a charm of powerful trouble,
Like a hell-broth boil and bubble.

SECOND WITCH

Cool it with a baboon's blood,
Then the charm is firm and good.

William Shakespeare

The Witch

I have walked a great while over the snow,
And I am not tall nor strong.
My clothes are wet, and my teeth are set,
And the way was hard and long.
I have wandered over the fruitful earth,
But I never came here before.
Oh, lift me over the threshold, and let me in at
the door!

The cutting wind is a cruel foe.
I dare not stand in the blast.
My hands are stone, and my voice a groan,
And the worst of death is past.
I am but a little maiden still,
My little white feet are sore.
Oh, lift me over thc thrcshold, and let me in at
the door!

Her voice was the voice that women have,
Who plead for their heart's desire.
She came—she came—and the quivering
flame
Sank and died in the fire.

It never was lit again on my hearth
Since I hurried across the floor,
To lift her over the threshold, and let her in at
  the door.

Mary Elizabeth Coleridge

The White Witch

O brothers mine, take care! Take care!
The great white witch rides out to-night.
Trust not your prowess nor your strength,
Your only safety lies in flight;
For in her glance there is a snare,
And in her smile there is a blight.

The great white witch you have not seen?
Then, younger brothers mine, forsooth,
Like nursery children you have looked
For ancient hag and snaggle-tooth;
But no, not so; the witch appears
In all the glowing charms of youth.

Her lips are like carnations, red,
Her face like new-born lilies, fair,
Her eyes like ocean waters, blue,
She moves with subtle grace and air,
And all about her head there floats
The golden glory of her hair.

But though she always thus appears
In form of youth and mood of mirth,

Unnumbered centuries are hers,
The infant planets saw her birth;
The child of throbbing Life is she,
Twin sister to the greedy earth.

And back behind those smiling lips,
And down within those laughing eyes,
And underneath the soft caress
Of hand and voice and purring sighs,
The shadow of the panther lurks,
The spirit of the vampire lies.

For I have seen the great white witch,
And she has led me to her lair,
And I have kissed her red, red lips
And cruel face so white and fair;
Around me she has twined her arms,
And bound me with her yellow hair.

I felt those red lips burn and sear
My body like a living coal;
Obeyed the power of those eyes
As the needle trembles to the pole;
And did not care although I felt
The strength go ebbing from my soul.

Oh! she has seen your strong young limbs,
And heard your laughter loud and gay,
And in your voices she has caught
The echo of a far-off day,
When man was closer to the earth;
And she has marked you for her prey.

She feels the old Antaean strength
In you, the great dynamic beat
Of primal passions, and she sees
In you the last besieged retreat
Of love relentless, lusty, fierce,
Love pain-ecstatic, cruel-sweet.

O, brothers mine, take care! Take care!
The great white witch rides out to-night.
O, younger brothers mine, beware!
Look not upon her beauty bright;
For in her glance there is a snare,
And in her smile there is a blight.

James Weldon Johnson

from The Witch of Atlas

I.

Before those cruel twins, whom at one birth
    Incestuous Change bore to her father Time,
Error and Truth, had hunted from the earth
    All those bright natures which adorned its
        prime,
And left us nothing to believe in, worth
    The pains of putting into learned rhyme,
A lady-witch there lived on Atlas' mountain
Within a cavern by a secret fountain.

II.

Her mother was one of the Atlantides:
    The all-beholding Sun had ne'er beholden
In his wide voyage o'er continents and seas
    So fair a creature, as she lay enfolden
In the warm shadow of her loveliness;
    He kissed her with his beams, and made all
        golden
The chamber of grey rock in which she lay—
She, in that dream of joy, dissolved away.

III.

’Tis said, she was first changed into a vapour,
    And then into a cloud, such clouds as flit,
Like splendour-winged moths about a taper,
    Round the red west when the sun dies in it:
And then into a meteor, such as caper
    On hill-tops when the moon is in a fit;
Then, into one of those mysterious stars
Which hide themselves between the Earth and
  Mars.

IV.

Ten times the Mother of the Months had bent
    Her bow beside the folding-star, and
      bidden
With that bright sign the billows to indent
    The sea-deserted sand: like children
      chidden,
At her command they ever came and went:—
    Since in that cave a dewy splendour
      hidden,
Took shape and motion: with the living form
Of this embodied Power, the cave grew warm.

V.

A lovely lady garmented in light
From her own beauty—deep her eyes, as are
Two openings of unfathomable night
Seen through a tempest's cloven roof;—her hair
Dark—the dim brain whirls dizzy with delight,
Picturing her form;–her soft smiles shone afar,
And her low voice was heard like love, and drew
All living things towards this wonder new.

Percy Shelley

from Paradise Lost

As when far off at Sea a Fleet descry'd
Hangs in the Clouds, by *Æquinoctial* Winds
Close failing from *Bengala*, or the Isles
Of *Ternate* and *Tidore*, whence Merchants
  bring
Their spicy Drugs: they on the Trading Floud
Through the wide *Ethiopian* to the Cape
Ply stemming nightly toward the Pole. So
  seem'd
Farr off the flying Fiend: at last appear
Hell bounds high reaching to the horrid Roof,
And thrice threefold the Gates; three folds were
  Brass,
Three Iron, three of Adamantine Rock,
Impenetrable, impal'd with circling fire,
Yet-unconsum'd. Before the Gates there sate
On either side a formidable shape;
The one seem'd Woman to the waste, and fair,
But ended foul in many a scaly fould
Voluminous and vast, a Serpent arm'd
With mortal sting: about her middle round
A cry of Hell Hounds never ceasing bark'd

With wide *Cerberian* mouths full loud, and rung
A hideous Peal: yet, when they list, would creep,
If aught disturb'd their noise, into her womb,
And kennel there, yet there still bark'd and howl'd,
Within unseen. Far less abhorr'd than these
Vex'd *Scylla* bathing in the Sea that parts
Calabria from the hoarse *Trinacrian* shore:
Nor uglier follow the Night-Hag, when call'd
In secret, riding through the Air she comes
Lur'd with the smell of infant bloud, to dance
With *Lapland* Witches, while the labouring Moon
Eclipses at their charms. The other shape,
If shape it might be call'd, that shape had none
Distinguishable in member, joynt or limb,
Or substance might be call'd, that shadow seem'd,
For each seem'd either; black it stood as Night,
Fierce as ten Furies, terrible as Hell,

And shook a dreadfull Dart; what seem'd his
head
The likeness of a Kingly Crown had on.
Satan was now at hand, and from his seat
The Monster moving onward came as fast
With horrid strides, Hell trembled as he strode.

John Milton

from The Witch

Al. Sweet venery be with thee, and I at the
taile
Of my wish! I am a litle head-strong, and soe
Are most of the company. I will to the witches.
They say they have charmes and tricks to make
A wench fall backwards, and lead a man herself
To a cuntry-house some mile out of the towne,
Like a fire-drake. There be such whorson kind
Girles, and such bawdy witches, and I'll try
Conclusions.

Thomas Middleton

The Hag

The Hag is astride,
This night for to ride;
The Devill and shee together:
Through thick, and through thin,
Now out, and then in,
Though ne'r so foule be the weather.

A Thorn or a Burr
She takes for a Spurre:
With a lash of a Bramble she rides now,
Through Brakes and through
Bryars,
O're Ditches, and Mires,
She followes the Spirit that guides
now.

No Beast, for his food,
Dares now range the wood;
But husht in his laire he lies lurking:
While mischeifs, by these,
On Land and on Seas,
At noone of Night are a working.

The storme will arise,
And trouble the skies;
This night, and more for the wonder,
The ghost from the Tomb
Affrighted shall come,
Cal'd out by the clap of the Thunder.

Robert Herrick

from The Masque of Queens

"The owl is abroad, the bat, and the toad,
    And so is the cat-a-mountain,
The ant and the mole sit both in a hole,
    And frog peeps out o' the fountain;
The dogs they do bay, and the timbrels play,
The spindle is now a turning;
    The moon it is red, and the stars are fled,
    But all the sky is a burning:
The ditch is made, and our nails the spade,
With pictures full of wax and of wool;
Their livers I stick with needles quick;
There lacks but the blood, to make up the flood.
    Quickly, dame, then bring your part in,
    Spur, spur upon little Martin,
Merrily, merrily, make him sail,
A worm in his mouth, and a thorn in 's tail,
Fire above and fire below,
With a whip i' your hand to make him go."

Ben Jonson

from The Witch of Edmonton

M. Saw. Why, then, on me,
Or any lean old beldam? Reverence once
Had wont to wait on age; now an old
woman,
Ill-favoured grown with years, if she be poor,
Must be called bawd or witch. Such so
abused
Are the coarse witches; t'other are the fine,
Spun for the devil's own wearing.
Sir Arth. And so is thine.
M. Saw. She on whose tongue a
whirlwind sits to blow
A man out of himself, from his soft pillow
To lean his head on rocks and fighting
waves,
Is not that scold a witch? The man of law
Whose honeyed hopes the credulous client
draw—
As bees by tinkling basins—to swarm to him
From his own hive to work the wax in his;
He is no witch, not he!
Sir Arth. But these men-witches
Are not in trading with hell's merchandise,

Like such as you are, that for a word, a look,
Denial of a coal of fire, kill men,
Children, and cattle.

William Rowley, Thomas Dekker, John Ford

The Elder-Witch

Though tall the oak, and firm its stem,
  Though far abroad its boughs are spread,
  Though high the poplar lifts its head,
I have no song for them.
  A theme more bright, more bright would be
  The winsome, winsome elder tree,
Beneath whose shade I sit reclin'd;—
  It holds a witch within its bark,
  A lovely witch who haunts the dark,
And fills with love my mind.

When ghosts, at midnight, leave their graves,
  And rous'd is every phantom thing;
  When mermaids rise and sweetly sing
In concert with the waves;
  When Palnatoka, on his steed,
  Pursues the elves across the mead,
Or gallops, gallops o'er the sea,
  The witch within the elder's bark,
  The lovely witch who haunts the dark,
Comes out, comes out to me.

Of leaves the fairies make our bed;
  The knight, who moulders 'neath the elm,
  Starts up with spear and rusted helm,—
By him the grace is said;
  And though her kiss is cold at times,
  And does not scent of earthly climes,
Though glaring is her eye, yet still
  The witch within the elder's bark,
  The lovely witch who haunts the dark,
I prize, and ever will.

Yet, once I lov'd a mortal maid,
  And gaz'd, enraptur'd, on her charms,
  Oft circled in each other's arms,
Together, here we stray'd;—
  But, soon, she found a fairer youth,
  And I a fairer maid, forsooth !
And one more true, more true to me,
  The witch within the elder's bark,
  The lovely witch who haunts the dark,
Has been more true to me.

George Borrow

from Tam O'Shanter

Inspiring bold John Barleycorn!
What dangers thou canst make us scorn!
Wi' tippenny we fear nae evil;
Wi' usquebae we'll face the Devil!—
The swats sae reamed in Tammie's noddle,
Fair play, he cared na Deils a bodle.
But Maggie stood right sair astonished,
Till, by the heel and hand admonished,
She ventured forward on the light;
And, wow! Tam saw an unco sight!
Warlocks and witches in a dance:
Nae cotillon brent new frae France,
But hornpipes, jigs, strathspeys, and reels
Put life and mettle in their heels.
A winnock-bunker in the east,
There sat auld Nick, in shape o' beast,—
A towzie tyke, black, grim, and large,—
To gie them music was his charge;
He screwed the pipes and gart them skirl
Till roof an' rafter a' did dirl.
Coffins stood round like open presses,
That shawed the dead in their last dresses;
And by some devilish cantrip sleight,

Each in its cauld hand held a light,—
By which heroic Tam was able
To note, upon the haly table,
A murderer's banes in gibbet airns;
Twa span-lang, wee, unchristened bairns;
A thief, new cutted frae a rape,
Wi' his last gasp his gab did gape;
Five tomahawks, wi' bluid red rusted;
Five scymitars, wi' murder crusted;
A garter which a babe had strangled;
A knife a father's throat had mangled,
Whom his ain son o' life bereft,—
The gray hairs yet stack to the heft;
Three lawyers' tongues turned inside out,
Wi' lies seamed like a beggar's clout;
And priests' hearts, rotten, black as muck,
Lay stinking, vile, in every neuk:
Wi' mair o' horrible and awfu'
Which even to name wad be unlawfu'.

Robert Burns

Witch-Burning

They burned a witch in Bingham Square
  Last Friday afternoon.
The faggot-smoke was blacker than
  The shadows on the moon;
The licking flames were strangely green
  Like fox-fire on the fen . . .
And she who cursed the godly folk
  Will never curse again.

They burned a witch in Bingham Square
  Before the village gate.
A huswife raised a skinny hand
  To damn her, tense with hate.
A huckster threw a jagged stone—
  Her pallid cheek ran red . . .
But there was something scornful in
  The way she held her head.

They burned a witch in Bingham Square;
  Her eyes were terror-wild.
She was a slight, a comely maid,
  No taller than a child.

They bound her fast against the stake
  And laughed to see her fear . . .
Her red lips muttered secret words
  That no one dared to hear.

They burned a witch in Bingham Square—
  But ere she swooned with pain
And ere her bones were sodden ash
  Beneath the sudden rain,
She set her mark upon that throng . . .
  For time can not erase
The echo of her anguished cries,
The memory of her face.

Mary Elizabeth Counselman

Witch

We are the blood
of the witches
you thought were dead.

We carry witchcraft in our bones
whilst the magic still sings
inside our heads.

When the witch hunters
imprisoned our ancestors
when they tried to burn the magic away.

Someone should have
warned them
that magic cannot be tamed.

Because you cannot burn away
what has always
been aflame.

Nikita Gill

Fairies & Goblins

A Flutter of Fairies

Collected by Clare

A flutter of fairies.
A whisper of wings.
A shiver of cobwebs.
A spangle of rings.
A canter of horse flies.
A rumble of bees.
A splatter of frogs.
A city of trees.
A village of toadstools.
An ocean of ponds.
A procession of snails.
A sparkle of wands.
A glimmer of glow-worms.
A treasure of dew.
A shower of wishes
For me. And for you.

Clare Bevan

Fairy Bread

Come up here, O dusty feet!
  Here is fairy bread to eat.
Here in my retiring room,
  Children, you may dine
On the golden smell of broom
  And the shade of pine;
And when you have eaten well,
Fairy stories hear and tell.

Robert Louis Stevenson

The Faëry Forest

The faëry forest glimmered
  Beneath an ivory moon,
The silver grasses shimmered
  Against a faëry tune.

Beneath the silken silence
  The crystal branches slept,
And dreaming through the dew-fall
  The cold, white blossoms wept.

Sara Teasdale

from A Midsummer Night's Dream

PUCK

How now, spirit! whither wander you?

FAIRY

Over hill, over dale,
Thorough bush, thorough brier,
Over park, over pale,
Thorough flood, thorough fire,
I do wander every where,
Swifter than the moon's sphere;
And I serve the fairy queen,
To dew her orbs upon the green.
The cowslips tall her pensioners be:
In their gold coats spots you see;
Those be rubies, fairy favours,
In those freckles live their savours:

I must go seek some dewdrops here,
And hang a pearl in every cowslip's ear.

Farewell, thou lob of spirits; I'll be gone:
Our queen and all her elves come here anon.

William Shakespeare

Will-O'-Wisp

This elfin sprite, as ancient legends say,
Was fairy-born; on him they did bestow
The art to lead poor villagers astray,
For an offence some thousand years ago.
This elfin sprite with meteor lantern hies
Close to the edge of slimy pool or lake;
Still like an anxious guide before them flies,
Nor, till some mischief done, does them forsake.
This elfin sprite have many tried to seize,
Yet in the rash attempt have suffer'd sore;
With mockery of himself he will them teize,
Which grasping hard, they see him still before.

Then on to fairy land, in gay despight,
Upon a zephyr will this elfin ride;
And all the fays do at his lantern light
Their little torches, and the feast provide.
Now seated round the tulip's ample bowl,
To jocund elves he doth his wiles betray;
In mirthful glee the hours unheeded roll,
Till dawn just peeps, then swift they hie away.

Charlotte Dacre

The Faëry Chasm

No fiction was it of the antique age:
A sky-blue stone, within this sunless cleft,
Is of the very foot-marks unbereft
Which tiny Elves impressed;—on that smooth stage
Dancing with all their brilliant equipage
In secret revels—haply after theft
Of some sweet Babe—Flower stolen, and coarse Weed left
For the distracted Mother to assuage
Her grief with, as she might!—But, where, oh! where
Is traceable a vestige of the notes
That ruled those dances wild in character?—
Deep underground? Or in the upper air,
On the shrill wind of midnight? or where floats
O'er twilight fields the autumnal gossamer?

William Wordsworth

from Thomas the Rhymer

True Thomas lay on Huntlie bank:
  A ferlie he spied wi' his e'e;
And there he saw a ladye bright,
  Come riding down by the Eildon Tree.

Her skirt was o' the grass-green silk,
  Her mantle o' the velvet fyne;
At ilka tett of her horse's mane,
  Hang fifty siller bells and nine.

True Thomas he pulled aff his cap,
  And louted low down to his knee,—
"All hail, thou mighty queen of heaven!
  For thy peer on earth I never did see."

"O no, O no, Thomas," she said;
  "That name does not belang to me;
I am but the queen of fair Elfland,
  That am hither come to visit thee.

"Harp and carp, Thomas," she said;
  "Harp and carp along with me;
And if ye dare to kiss my lips,
  Sure of your bodie I will be."

"Betide me weal, betide me wo,
  That weird shall never danton me."
Syne he has kissed her rosy lips,
  All underneath the Eildon Tree.

"Now ye maun go wi' me," she said;
  "True Thomas, ye maun go wi' me
And ye maun serve me seven years,
  Through weal or wo as may chance to be."

She mounted on her milk-white steed;
  She's ta'en true Thomas up behind;
And aye, whene'er her bridle rung,
  The steed flew swifter than the wind.

O they rade on, and farther on;
  The steed gaed swifter than the wind;
Until they reached a desart wide,
  And living land was left behind.

“Light down, light down, now, true Thomas,
And lean your head upon my knee;
Abide, and rest a little space,
And I will show you ferlies three.

“O see ye not yon narrow road,
So thick beset with thorns and briers?—
That is the path of righteousness,
Though after it but few inquires.

“And see not ye that braid, braid road,
That lies across that lily leven?—
That is the path of wickedness,
Though some call it the road to heaven.

“And see not ye that bonny road,
That winds about the fernie brae?
That is the road to fair Elfland,
Where thou and I this night maun gae.

“But, Thomas, ye maun hold your tongue,
Whatever ye may hear or see;
For, if you speak word in Elflyn land,
Ye’ll ne’er get back to your ain countrie.”

O they rade on, and farther on,
And they waded through rivers aboon the knee,
And they saw neither sun nor moon,
But they heard the roaring of the sea.

It was mirk, mirk night, and there was nae starn light,
And they waded through red blude to the knee;
For a' the blude that's shed on earth,
Rins through the springs o' that countrie.

Syne they came on to a garden green,
And she pu'd an apple frae a tree—
"Take this for thy wages, true Thomas;
It will give thee the tongue that can never lie."

"My tongue is mine ain," true Thomas said;
"A gudely gift ye wad gie to me!
I neither dought to buy nor sell,
At fair or tryst, where I may be.

"I dought neither speak to prince or peer,
  Nor ask of grace from fair ladye."
"Now hold thy peace!" the ladye said,
  "For, as I say, so must it be."

He has gotten a coat of the even cloth,
  And a pair of shoes of velvet green;
And, till seven years were gane and past,
  True Thomas on earth was never seen.

Sir Walter Scott

from Goblin Market

Morning and evening
Maids heard the goblins cry:
"Come buy our orchard fruits,
Come buy, come buy:
Apples and quinces,
Lemons and oranges,
Plump unpecked cherries,
Melons and raspberries,
Bloom-down-cheeked peaches,
Swart-headed mulberries,
Wild free-born cranberries,
Crab-apples, dewberries,
Pine-apples, blackberries,
Apricots, strawberries;—
All ripe together
In summer weather,—
Morns that pass by,
Fair eves that fly;
Come buy, come buy:
Our grapes fresh from the vine,
Pomegranates full and fine,
Dates and sharp bullaces,
Rare pears and greengages,

Damsons and bilberries,
Taste them and try:
Currants and gooseberries,
Bright-fire-like barberries,
Figs to fill your mouth,
Citrons from the South,
Sweet to tongue and sound to eye;
Come buy, come buy."
Evening by evening
Among the brookside rushes,
Laura bowed her head to hear,
Lizzie veiled her blushes:
Crouching close together
In the cooling weather,
With clasping arms and cautioning lips,
With tingling cheeks and finger tips.
"Lie close," Laura said,
Pricking up her golden head:
"We must not look at goblin men,
We must not buy their fruits:
Who knows upon what soil they fed
Their hungry thirsty roots?"
"Come buy," call the goblins
Hobbling down the glen.

Christina Rossetti

The Nine Little Goblins

They all climbed up on a high board-fence—
Nine little goblins, with green-glass eyes—
Nine little goblins that had no sense,
And couldn't tell coppers from cold
mince-pies;
And they all climbed up on the fence, and
sat—
And I asked them what they were
staring at.

And the first one said, as he scratched his head
With a queer little arm that reached out of
his ear
And rasped its claws in his hair so red—
"This is what this little arm is fer!"
And he scratched and stared, and the
next one said,
"How on earth do *you* scratch your
head?"

And he laughed like the screech of a rusty
  hinge—
    Laughed and laughed till his face grew
      black;
And when he choked, with a final twinge
    Of his stifling laughter, he thumped his
      back
        With a fist that grew on the end of his
          tail
        Till the breath came back to his lips so
          pale.

And the third little goblin leered round at me—
    And there were no lids on his eyes at all—
And he clucked one eye, and he says, says he,
    "What is the style of your socks this fall?"
        And he clapped his heels—and I
          sighed to see
        That he had hands where his feet
          should be.

Then a bald-faced goblin, gray and grim,
    Bowed his head, and I saw him slip
His eyebrows off, as I looked at him,
    And paste them over his upper lip;

And then he moaned in remorseful
pain—
"Would—ah, would I'd me brows
again!"

And then the whole of the goblin band
Rocked on the fence-top to and fro,
And clung, in a long row, hand in hand,
Singing the songs that they used to know—
Singing the songs that their grandsires
sung
In the goo-goo days of the goblin-tongue.

And ever they kept their green-glass eyes
Fixed on me with a stony stare—
Till my own grew glazed with a dread surmise,
And my hat whooped up on my lifted hair,
And I felt the heart in my breast
snap to,
As you've heard the lid of a snuff-
box do.

And they sang: "You're asleep! There is no board fence,
And never a goblin with green-glass eyes!—
'Tis only a vision the mind invents
After a supper of cold mince-pies,—
And you're doomed to dream this way," they said,—
"And you shan't wake up till you're clean plum dead!"

James Whitcomb Riley

The Changeling

Toll no bell for me, dear Father, dear Mother,
    Waste no sighs;
There are my sisters, there is my little brother
    Who plays in the place called Paradise,
Your children all, your children for ever;
    But I, so wild,
Your disgrace, with the queer brown face, was never,
    Never, I know, but half your child!

In the garden at play, all day, last summer,
    Far and away I heard
The sweet "tweet-tweet" of a strange new-comer,
    The dearest, clearest call of a bird.
It lived down there in the deep green hollow,
    My own old home, and the fairies say
The word of a bird is a thing to follow,
    So I was away a night and a day.

One evening, too, by the nursery fire,
    We snuggled close and sat round so still,
When suddenly as the wind blew higher,
    Something scratched on the window-sill,
A pinched brown face peered in—I shivered;
    No one listened or seemed to see;
The arms of it waved and the wings of it
  quivered,
Whoo—I knew it had come for me!
    Some are as bad as bad can be!

All night long they danced in the rain,
Round and round in a dripping chain,
Threw their caps at the window-pane,
    Tried to make me scream and shout
    And fling the bedclothes all about:
I meant to stay in bed that night,
And if only you had left a light
    They would never have got me out!

    Sometimes I wouldn't speak, you see,
    Or answer when you spoke to me,
Because in the long, still dusks of Spring
You can hear the whole world whispering;
    The shy green grasses making love,

The feathers grow on the dear grey dove,
The tiny heart of the redstart beat,
The patter of the squirrel's feet,
The pebbles pushing in the silver streams,
The rushes talking in their dreams,
The swish-swish of the bat's black wings,
The wild-wood bluebell's sweet ting-tings,
Humming and hammering at your ear,
Everything there is to hear
In the heart of hidden things.
But not in the midst of the nursery riot.
That's why I wanted to be quiet,
Couldn't do my sums, or sing,
Or settle down to anything.
And when, for that, I was sent upstairs
I *did* kneel down to say my prayers;
But the King who sits on your high church steeple
Has nothing to do with us fairy people!

'Times I pleased you, dear Father, dear Mother,
Learned all my lessons and liked to play,
And dearly I loved the little pale brother
Whom some other bird must have called away.

Why did they bring me here to make me
    Not quite bad and not quite good,
Why, unless They're wicked, do They want, in spite, to take me
    Back to Their wet, wild wood?
Now, every night I shall see the windows shining,
    The gold lamp's glow, and the fire's red gleam,
While the best of us are twining twigs and the rest of us are whining
    In the hollow by the stream.
Black and chill are Their nights on the wold
    And They live so long and They feel no pain:
I shall grow up, but never grow old,
I shall always, always be very cold,
    I shall never come back again!

Charlotte Mew

from The Monastery

'What I am I must not show,
What I am thou couldst not know.
Something betwixt heaven and hell,
Something that neither stood nor fell,
Something that through thy wit or will
May work thee good—may work thee ill.
Neither substance quite nor shadow,
Haunting lonely moor and meadow,
Dancing by the haunted spring,
Riding on the whirlwind's wing;
Aping in fantastic fashion
Every change of human passion.
While o'er our frozen minds they pass,
Like shadows from the mirror'd glass.

Wayward, fickle is our mood,
Hovering betwixt bad and good,
Happier than brief-dated man,
Living twenty times his span;
Far less happy, for we have
Help nor hope beyond the grave!
Man awakes to joy or sorrow;

Ours the sleep that knows no morrow.
This is all that I can show—
This is all that thou mayest know.'

Sir Walter Scott

Somewhere in the World

Between the blue of a sparkling sea
And the azure of a summer sky,
The snow-white wings of fairy-terns
Filter sunlight as they fly.

Between the seaweed in sandy rock pools,
If you had the eyes of a hungry fish,
You might see the dainty fairy-shrimp
Dart out of reach to a rocky niche.

Between the blades of daisied grass
Where there's a stranger, darker green
Is the emerald mark of a fairy-ring,
Though no fairies can be seen.

Between the silver of the moon
And the street lamps' pools of golden light
When ghost-moths flitter, you might believe
You've seen fairies dance, and you may be right.

And – if you knew just where to look
And you made a promise not to tell
You might discover and make a wish
In the secret water of a fairy-well.

Catherine Benson

Dragons & Monsters

The Furies

Beneath the earth they wait   hissing
Deep in graves of dirt   listening
Blood-red eyes of hate   dripping

Each faithless man they take in turn
The violent husbands, liars, thieves
Ruled by lust, desire or greed
Are captured, never to return

With wings of bats unrolled   beating
Their skin is black as coal   glistening
Skulls with serpents coiled   shrieking

Torches, daggers, whips and knives
Teeming cups of poisoned drink
Nightmares issue from each wink
Justice is repaid with life

The vengeful sisters wait   unceasing
Administering their rage   believe it
So think before you play   or trick me

Lavinia Singer

The Kraken

Below the thunders of the upper deep;
Far, far beneath in the abysmal sea,
His ancient, dreamless, uninvaded sleep
The Kraken sleepeth: faintest sunlights flee
About his shadowy sides: above him swell
Huge sponges of millennial growth and height;
And far away into the sickly light,
From many a wondrous grot and secret cell
Unnumber'd and enormous polypi
Winnow with giant arms the slumbering green.
There hath he lain for ages and will lie
Battening upon huge seaworms in his sleep,
Until the latter fire shall heat the deep;
Then once by man and angels to be seen,
In roaring he shall rise and on the surface die.

Alfred, Lord Tennyson

Jabberwocky

'Twas brillig, and the slithy toves
  Did gyre and gimble in the wabe:
All mimsy were the borogoves,
  And the mome raths outgrabe.

'Beware the Jabberwock, my son!
  The jaws that bite, the claws that catch!
Beware the Jubjub bird, and shun
  The frumious Bandersnatch!'

He took his vorpal sword in hand;
  Long time the manxome foe he sought—
So rested he by the Tumtum tree
  And stood awhile in thought.

And, as in uffish thought he stood,
  The Jabberwock, with eyes of flame,
Came whiffling through the tulgey wood,
  And burbled as it came!

One, two! One, two! And through and through
  The vorpal blade went snicker-snack!
He left it dead, and with its head
  He went galumphing back.

'And hast thou slain the Jabberwock?
  Come to my arms, my beamish boy!
O frabjous day! Callooh! Callay!'
  He chortled in his joy.

'Twas brillig, and the slithy toves
  Did gyre and gimble in the wabe:
All mimsy were the borogoves,
  And the mome raths outgrabe.

Lewis Carroll

The Dragon and the Undying

All night the flares go up; the Dragon sings
And beats upon the dark with furious wings;
And, stung to rage by his own darting fires,
Reaches with grappling coils from town to town;
He lusts to break the loveliness of spires,
And hurls their martyred music toppling down.

Yet, though the slain are homeless as the breeze,
Vocal are they, like storm-bewilder'd seas.
Their faces are the fair, unshrouded night,
And planets are their eyes, their ageless dreams.
Tenderly stooping earthward from their height,
They wander in the dusk with chanting streams;
And they are dawn-lit trees, with arms up-flung,
To hail the burning heavens they left unsung.

Siegfried Sassoon

from Beowulf

I.

HOW THE DRAGON GOT THE HOARD AND WASTED THE LAND

Then afterwards the kingdom wide passed
to Beowulf's hand.
He ruled it well for fifty years, old guardian of
the land,
And prudent king, till in dark nights began the
dragon's sway
Who in the high cliff kept the hoard, upon the
moorland grey;
Unknown to men the path below . . .
Great heaps of treasure of old time in that
earth-cavern lay,
The heritage of noble men, which he of olden
day,
I wot not who, with anxious care had hidden,—
treasures good.
Ere then had death swept all away, and sad was
he of mood
Who longest tarried there alone,—the last of
valiant men.

Delay he sought that yet awhile he might enjoy again
His treasure. Ready stood the hill, made strong by subtle lore,
Upon the plain, below the ness, hard by the billowy shore.
In it the guardian of the rings that lordly treasure laid,
A heavy load of plated gold, and dark the spell he said:
"O earth! keep thou the warriors' hoard which men may keep no more!
Lo! upon thee by valiant men 'twas gained in days of yore.
But war and death have swept away my comrades every one;
Of those who saw the joys of hall to wield the sword there's none,
Or fill the beaker goodly wrought. Gone are the brave elsewhere!
From frowning helmet dight with gold must fall the plating fair;
They sleep who would have kept it bright! The mail that bite of sword

O'er clashing shield in fight withstood must
follow its dead lord.
Never again shall corselet ring as help the
warriors bear
To comrades far! No joy of harp, no sound of
music there!
Around the hall no good hawk flies, in court no
coursers tread!
Before the baleful stroke of death all shapes of
life are fled!"
Thus mournfully he told his grief, and day and
night he wept,
Left lonely there till waves of death his sad
heart over-swept.
The goodly hoard was open found by that old
darkling foe
Who dwelleth flaming in the hills,—the dragon
bringing woe—
Who roams by night begirt with fire, by land-
folk far beheld.
There in the cavern shall he dwell to many
winters eld,
And guard therein the heathen gold—no whit
the better he!

Three hundred years beneath the earth the
  people's enemy
With mighty strength his hoard-house kept, till
  angered by the thrall
Who took the chased cup to his lord to make
  his peace withal.
Then was the treasure robbed, the hoard of
  rings was borne away,
And granted was the poor man's bene. Men's
  work of olden day
For the first time the lord beheld. But when the
  dragon woke
Was wrath renewed; the fierce of heart scented
  along the rock,
And found the footprints of the foe; for near
  the dragon's head
With stealthy craft his steps had gone. (Thus
  safe may he be led
From woes and pains whom God's grace keeps,
  as yet undoomed to die.)
Closely the hoard-ward searched the ground,
  the man to find thereby
Who while he slept had done him wrong, and
  hotly raging chased

Around the hill, but found him not in all the
heathy waste.
Yet eager for the bloody strife, back to the cave
he turned
To see his hoard, and quickly found a man the
way had learned
To that great wealth of gold. Then hardly would
the hoard-ward stay—
So wrath was he—till evening came, athirst that
men should pay
Dear for his drinking-cup with fire; and when
the day was spent,
Ev'n to his wish, no more in den would he
abide, but went,
With flames engirdled, blazing forth.
Like as beginning dread
To land-folk—soon the bitter end fell on their
leader's head!

Then spued the fiend out flames of fire and
burned the dwellings fair;
Baneful to men the lightnings flashed; the hate
that winged the air
Willed death to every living thing. Wide was his
bitter wrath

And slaughter seen; and far and near that scather of the Goth
Wronged them with hatred—brought them low—and then ere break of day
Betook him to his hoard again in secret hall that lay.
The land-folk had he girt with fire and burning brand and bale,
Trusting his stronghold and his might; him nought did they avail!
Then to Beowulf sooth and swift the dreadful tidings came
That his fair hall, gift-seat of Goths, was burnt in waves of flame.
This worst of griefs his kindly heart with bitter sorrow tore;
The wise king weened that God eternal he had angered sore
By sin against the old command; and in his breast awoke
Dark thoughts that were not wont with him. The stronghold of the folk,
The isle beyond, and all the land, the fiery drake had burned.

The Weder chief, the warrior king, his mind to
  vengeance turned.
A wondrous shield the lord of earls bade make
  of iron good,
For well he knew that 'gainst the flames no
  help was linden wood.
The end of life's lent days on earth the good
  prince must abide,
And with him too the worm, though long the
  hoard had he enjoyed.
The ring-bestower scorned to seek with host
  and great array
The wide-winged dragon; never yet did battle
  him affray,
And nothing recked he of his foe his valour and
  his might.

Anon. tr. Lumsden

from The Dragon of Wantley

Old stories tell, how Hercules
A dragon slew at Lerna,
With seven heads, and fourteen eyes,
To see and well discern-a:
But he had a club, this dragon to drub,
Or he had ne'er done it, I warrant ye:
But More of More-Hall, with nothing at all,
He slew the dragon of Wantley.

This dragon had two furious wings,
Each one upon each shoulder;
With a sting in his tayl, as long as a flayl,
Which made him bolder and bolder.
He had long claws, and in his jaws
Four and forty teeth of iron;
With a hide as tough as any buff,
Which did him round environ.

Anon.

from St. George and the Dragon

Now, as the story plain doth tell,
  Within that countrey there did rest
A dreadful dragon fierce and fell,
  Whereby they were full sore opprest:
Who by his poisonous breath each day,
Did many of the city slay.

The grief whereof did grow so great
  Throughout the limits of the land,
That they their wise-men did intreat
  To shew their cunning out of hand;
What way they might this fiend destroy,
That did the countrey thus annoy.

The wise-men all before the king
  This answer fram'd incontinent;
The dragon none to death might bring
  By any means they could invent:
His skin more hard than brass was found,
That sword nor spear could pierce nor wound.

When this the people understood,
  They cryed out most piteouslye,

The dragon's breath infects their blood,
  That every day in heaps they dye:
Among them such a plague it bred,
The living scarce could bury the dead.

No means there were, as they could hear,
  For to appease the dragon's rage,
But to present some virgin clear,
  Whose blood his fury might asswage;
Each day he would a maiden eat,
For to allay his hunger great.

This thing by art the wise-men found,
  Which truly must observèd be;
Wherefore throughout the city round
  A virgin purc of good degree
Was by the king's commission still
Taken up to serve the dragon's will.

Thus did the dragon every day
  Untimely crop some virgin flowr,
Till all the maids were worn away,
  And none were left him to devour:
Saving the king's fair daughter bright,
Her father's only heart's delight.

Then came the officers to the king
  That heavy message to declare,
Which did his heart with sorrow sting;
  She is, quoth he, my kingdom's heir:
O let us all be poisoned here,
Ere she should die, that is my dear.

Then rose the people presently,
  And to the king in rage they went;
They said his daughter dear should dye,
  The dragon's fury to prevent:
Our daughters all are dead, quoth they,
And have been made the dragon's prey:

And by their blood we rescued were,
  And thou hast sav'd thy life thereby;
And now in sooth it is but faire,
  For us thy daughter so should die.
O save my daughter, said the king;
And let ME feel the dragon's sting.

Then fell fair Sabra on her knee,
  And to her father dear did say,
O father, strive not thus for me,
  But let me be the dragon's prey;

It may be, for my sake alone
This plague upon the land was thrown.

'Tis better I should dye, she said,
  Than all your subjects perish quite;
Perhaps the dragon here was laid,
  For my offence to work his spite:
And after he hath suckt my gore,
Your land shall feel the grief no more.

What hast thou done, my daughter dear,
  For to deserve this heavy scourge?
It is my fault, as may appear,
  Which makes the gods our state to purge;
Then ought I die, to stint the strife,
And to preserve thy happy life.

Like mad-men, all the people cried,
  Thy death to us can do no good;
Our safety only doth abide
  In making her the dragon's food.
Lo! here I am, I come, quoth she,
Therefore do what you will with me.

Anon.

from The Raven

Once upon a midnight dreary, while I
pondered, weak and weary,
Over many a quaint and curious volume of
forgotten lore—
While I nodded, nearly napping, suddenly there
came a tapping,
As of some one gently rapping, rapping at my
chamber door;
"'Tis some visitor," I muttered, "tapping at my
chamber door—
Only this, and nothing more."

Ah! distinctly I remember it was in the bleak
December,
And each separate dying ember wrought its
ghost upon the floor.
Eagerly I wished the morrow;—vainly I had
sought to borrow
From my books surcease of sorrow—sorrow for
the lost Lenore
For the rare and radiant maiden whom the
angels name Lenore—
Nameless here for evermore.

And the silken sad uncertain rustling of each purple curtain
Thrilled me—filled me with fantastic terrors never felt before;
So that now, to still the beating of my heart, I stood repeating—
"'Tis some visitor entreating entrance at my chamber door:
Some late visitor entreating entrance at my chamber door,
This it is, and nothing more."

Presently my soul grew stronger; hesitating then no longer,
"Sir," said I, "or Madam, truly your forgiveness I implore;
But the fact is I was napping, and so gently you came rapping,
And so faintly you came tapping, tapping at my chamber door,
That I scarce was sure I heard you"—here I opened wide the door:—
Darkness there, and nothing more.

Deep into that darkness peering, long I stood
there, wondering, fearing,
Doubting, dreaming dreams no mortal ever
dared to dream before:
But the silence was unbroken, and the stillness
gave no token,
And the only word there spoken was the
whispered word "Lenore!"
This I whispered, and an echo murmured back
the word "Lenore!"
Merely this, and nothing more.

Back into the chamber turning, all my soul
within me burning,
Soon again I heard a tapping something louder
than before.
"Surely," said I, "surely that is something at my
window lattice;
Let me see, then, what thereat is, and this
mystery explore—
Let my heart be still a moment, and this
mystery explore:—
'Tis the wind, and nothing more.

Open here I flung the shutter, when, with many
  a flirt and flutter,
In there stepped a stately Raven of the saintly
  days of yore.
Not the least obeisance made he; not a minute
  stopped or stayed he;
But, with mien of lord or lady, perched above
  my chamber door—
Perched upon a bust of Pallas, just above my
  chamber door—
        Perched and sat, and nothing more.

Then this ebony bird beguiling my sad fancy
  into smiling,
By the grave and stern decorum of the
  countenance it wore,
"Though thy crest be shorn and shaven, thou,"
  I said, "art sure no craven.
Ghastly, grim, and ancient Raven wandering
  from the nightly shore—
Tell me what thy lordly name is on the night's
  Plutonian shore?"
        Quoth the Raven, "Nevermore."

Much I marvelled this ungainly fowl to hear
discourse so plainly,
Though its answer little meaning—little
relevancy bore;
For we cannot help agreeing that no living
human being
Ever yet was blessed with seeing bird above his
chamber door—
Bird or beast upon the sculptured bust above
his chamber door,
With such name as "Nevermore."

But the Raven, sitting lonely on that placid
bust, spoke only
That one word, as if his soul in that one word
he did outpour.
Nothing further then he uttered; not a feather
then he fluttered—
Till I scarcely more than muttered, "Other
friends have flown before—
On the morrow *he* will leave me, as my hopes
have flown before."
Then the bird said, "Never more."

Startled at the stillness broken by reply so aptly
spoken,
"Doubtless", said I, "what it utters is its only
stock and store,
Caught from some unhappy master, whom
unmerciful disaster
Followed fast and followed faster, till his songs
one burden bore—
Till the dirges of his hope that melancholy
burden bore,
Of 'Never—never more.'"

Edgar Allan Poe

Dryads

When meadows are grey with the morn,
In the dusk of the woods it is night;
The oak and the ash and the pine
War with the glimmer of light.

Dryads brown as the leaf
Move in the gloom of the glade;
When meadows are grey with the morn,
Dim night in the wood has delayed.

The cocks that crow to the land
Are faint and hollow and shrill:
Dryads as brown as the leaf
Whisper and hide and are still.

Siegfried Sassoon

The Kelpie of Loch Coruisk

In the morning, a milky sun
peeks over the spear-tips of the mountain.
Two infant clouds chase each other
across an ocean of sky.

This is the kind of day that
the Kelpie of Loch Coruisk loves.
A green sea-wind on his snowdrop-white blaze,
a warm sun on his rock-black back.

The wash and whine of the sea is his orchestra:
the gulls, the seals, the gannets
unite in song to become his choir.
And on a slab of sparkling rock, he dances.

This is no jittering Scottish jig, no rushing Irish reel.
This is a fast-flowing, watery wave of a dance –
a hoof-to-the-heavens swirling, swishing, sweeping
surge of a dance, a defiant devil of a dance!

Ho, there's no stopping him! He's off across
the loch's cold water, full speed down the glen,
skimming the rocky scree, disappearing over
the sharpest peak in a sound like cracking wood.

This is the kind of day that the
Kelpie of Loch Coruisk loves.
A day when dancing can be fun and joyful.
A day when he gets time off from drowning
people.

John Rice

Mermaid, Dragon, Fiend

In my childhood rumours ran
  Of a world beyond the door—
Terrors to the life of man
  That the highroad held in store.

Of the mermaids' doleful game
  In deep water I heard tell,
Of lofty dragons puffing flame,
  Of the hornèd fiend of Hell.

Tales like these were too absurd
  For my laughter-loving ear:
Soon I mocked at all I heard,
  Though with cause indeed for fear.

Now I know the mermaid kin
  I find them bound by natural laws:
They have neither tail nor fin,
  But are deadlier for that cause.

Dragons have no darting tongues,
  Teeth saw-edged nor rattling scales,

No fire issues from their lungs,
  No black poison from their tails:

For they are creatures of dark air,
  Unsubstantial tossing forms,
Thunderclaps of man's despair
  In mid-whirl of mental storms.

And there's a true and only fiend
  Worse than prophets prophesy,
Whose full powers to hurt are screened
  Lest the race of man should die.

Ever in vain will courage plot
  The dragon's death, in coat of proof;
Or love abjure the mermaid grot;
  Or faith denounce the cloven hoof.

Mermaids will not be denied
  The last bubbles of our shame,
The dragon flaunts an unpierced hide,
  The true fiend governs in God's name.

Robert Graves

Medusa and Minotaur Take Tea

The china is in smithereens
before our tea has even brewed
but it hardly matters.
Minotaur is half bull
and a little clumsy
but bigger things have been shattered,
like our reputations,
and we are here with pen and paper
to set the record straight.

We blame the poets
and the storytellers
and the kings playing at war
who wanted this head and that head,
this pesky soldier
and that far-off monster dead.
Often they didn't even leave their thrones.

'I didn't even like the taste
of human flesh, but it was all they sent
into the Labyrinth,' lows Minotaur.
I write this down,

and also that I didn't choose
to have a head of thrashing snakes,
to turn everyone who looks at me to stone.

The poets didn't care to judge
the malice heaped on us
by petty gods,
just how we ended up
and our ability to finish off
their 'heroes' Perseus and Theseus,
men we'd never heard of,
coming with swords and shields to kill us.
Wouldn't *you* put up a fight?
But of course it was useless.
In stories, monsters always die.

I get some sturdier mugs and pour the tea.
My hair hisses and seethes.
Minotaur asks me to write down
that we were lonely.

Rachel Piercey

Moon & Stars

A Hymn to the Moon

Written in July, in an arbour.

Thou silver deity of secret night,
    Direct my footsteps through the woodland
      shade;
Thou conscious witness of unknown delight,
    The Lover's guardian, and the Muse's aid!

By thy pale beams I solitary rove,
    To thee my tender grief confide;
Serenely sweet you gild the silent grove,
    My friend, my goddess, and my guide.

E'en thee, fair queen, from thy amazing height,
    The charms of young Endymion drew;
Veil'd with the mantle of concealing night;
    With all thy greatness and thy coldness too.

Lady Mary Wortley Montagu

The half moon shows a face of plaintive sweetness

The half moon shows a face of plaintive
sweetness
Ready and poised to wax or wane;
A fire of pale desire in incompleteness,
Tending to pleasure or to pain:—
Lo, while we gaze she rolleth on in fleetness
To perfect loss or perfect gain.
Half bitterness we know, we know half
sweetness;
This world is all on wax, on wane:
When shall completeness round time's
incompleteness,
Fulfilling joy, fulfilling pain?—
Lo, while we ask, life rolleth on in fleetness
To finished loss or finished gain.

Christina Rossetti

To the Moon

I.

Art thou pale for weariness
Of climbing Heaven and gazing on the earth,
Wandering companionless
Among the stars that have a different birth,—
And ever changing, like a joyless eye
That finds no object worth its constancy?

II.

Thou chosen sister of the spirit,
That gazes on thee till in thee it pities

Percy Shelley

The moon was but a chin of gold

The moon was but a chin of gold
  A night or two ago,
And now she turns her perfect face
  Upon the world below.

Her forehead is of amplest blond;
  Her cheek like beryl stone;
Her eye unto the summer dew
  The likest I have known.

Her lips of amber never part;
  But what must be the smile
Upon her friend she could bestow
  Were such her silver will!

And what a privilege to be
  But the remotest star!
For certainly her way might pass
  Beside your twinkling door.

Her bonnet is the firmament,
  The universe her shoe,
The stars the trinkets at her belt,
  Her dimities of blue.

Emily Dickinson

The Moon

The moon has a face like the clock in the hall;
She shines on thieves on the garden wall,
On streets and fields and harbour quays,
And birdies asleep in the forks of the trees.

The squalling cat and the squeaking mouse,
The howling dog by the door of the house,
The bat that lies in bed at noon,
All love to be out by the light of the moon.

But all of the things that belong to the day
Cuddle to sleep to be out of her way;
And flowers and children close their eyes
Till up in the morning the sun shall arise.

Robert Louis Stevenson

Moonlight

As a pale phantom with a lamp
  Ascends some ruin's haunted stair,
So glides the moon along the damp
  Mysterious chambers of the air.

Now hidden in cloud, and now revealed,
  As if this phantom, full of pain,
Were by the crumbling walls concealed,
  And at the windows seen again.

Until at last, serene and proud
  In all the splendor of her light,
She walks the terraces of cloud,
  Supreme as Empress of the Night.

I look, but recognize no more
  Objects familiar to my view;
The very pathway to my door
  Is an enchanted avenue.

All things are changed. One mass of shade,
  The elm-trees drop their curtains down;
By palace, park, and colonnade
  I walk as in a foreign town.

The very ground beneath my feet
  Is clothed with a diviner air;
While marble paves the silent street
  And glimmers in the empty square.

Illusion! Underneath there lies
  The common life of every day;
Only the spirit glorifies
  With its own tints the sober gray.

In vain we look, in vain uplift
  Our eyes to heaven, if we are blind;
We see but what we have the gift
  Of seeing; what we bring we find.

Henry Wadsworth Longfellow

When I heard the learn'd astronomer

When I heard the learn'd astronomer,
When the proofs, the figures, were ranged in
  columns before me,
When I was shown the charts and diagrams, to
  add, divide, and measure them,
When I sitting heard the astronomer where
  he lectured with much applause in the
  lecture-room,
How soon unaccountable I became tired and
  sick,
Till rising and gliding out I wander'd off by
  myself,
In the mystical moist night-air, and from time
  to time
Looked up in perfect silence at the stars.

Walt Whitman

To the Evening Star

Thou fair-haired Angel of the Evening,
Now, whilst the sun rests on the mountains,
  light
Thy bright torch of love: thy radiant crown
Put on, and smile upon our evening bed!
Smile on our loves: and, while thou drawest the
Blue curtains of the sky, scatter thy silver dew
On every flower that shuts its sweet eyes
In timely sleep. Let thy west wind sleep on
The lake: speak silence with thy glimmering
  eyes,
And wash the dusk with silver.—Soon, full
  soon,
Dost thou withdraw; then the wolf rages wide,
And then the lion glares through the dun forest.
The fleeces of our flocks are covered with
Thy sacred dew: protect them with thine
  influence!

William Blake

Stars

Alone in the night
   On a dark hill
With pines around me
   Spicy and still,

And a heaven full of stars
   Over my head,
White and topaz
   And misty red;

Myriads with beating
   Hearts of fire
That aeons
   Cannot vex or tire;

Up the dome of heaven
   Like a great hill,
I watch them marching
   Stately and still,

And I know that I
  Am honored to be
Witness
  Of so much majesty.

Sara Teasdale

Bright star, would I were stedfast as thou art

Written on a blank page in Shakespeare's poems, facing "A Lover's Complaint."

Bright star, would I were stedfast as thou art—
Not in lone splendour hung aloft the night
And watching, with eternal lids apart,
Like nature's patient, sleepless Eremite,
The moving waters at their priestlike task
Of pure ablution round earth's human shores,
Or gazing on the new soft-fallen mask
Of snow upon the mountains and the moors—
No—yet still stedfast, still unchangeable,
Pillow'd upon my fair love's ripening breast,
To feel for ever its soft fall and swell,
Awake for ever in a sweet unrest,
Still, still to hear her tender-taken breath,
And so live ever—or else swoon to death.

John Keats

Stars

Ah! why, because the dazzling sun
  Restored our Earth to joy,
Have you departed, every one
  And left a desert sky?

All through the night, your glorious eyes
  Were gazing down in mine,
And, with a full heart's thankful sighs,
  I blessed that watch divine.

I was at peace, and drank your beams
  As they were life to me;
And revelled in my changeful dreams,
  Like petrel on the sea.

Thought followed thought, star followed star,
  Through boundless regions, on;
While one sweet influence, near and far,
  Thrilled through, and proved us one!

Why did the morning dawn to break
  So great, so pure, a spell;
And scorch with fire the tranquil cheek,
  Where your cool radiance fell?

Blood-red, he rose, and arrow-straight,
  His fierce beams struck my brow;
The soul of nature sprang, elate,
  But *mine* sank sad and low!

My lids closed down, yet through their veil
  I saw him blazing, still,
And steep in gold the misty dale,
  And flash upon the hill.

I turned me to the pillow, then,
  To call back night, and see
Your worlds of solemn light, again,
  Throb with my heart, and me!

It would not do—the pillow glowed,
  And glowed both roof and floor;
And birds sang loudly in the wood,
  And fresh winds shook the door;

The curtains waved, the wakened flies
  Were murmuring round my room,
Imprisoned there, till I should rise,
  And give them leave to roam.

Oh, stars, and dreams, and gentle night;
  Oh, night and stars, return!
And hide me from the hostile light
  That does not warm, but burn;

That drains the blood of suffering men:
  Drinks tears, instead of dew;
Let me sleep through his blinding reign,
  And only wake with you!

Emily Brontë

Index of Poets and Authors

Permissions Acknowledgements

'Mermaid Becomes Merwife' © Gita Ralleigh from *Siren* (2022). Reproduced by permission of the author.

'The Mermaid's Garden' © Clare Bevan 2005. Reproduced by permission of the author.

'Witch' from *Wild Embers* by Nikita Gill © 2017. Reprinted by permission of Legacy Lit, an imprint of Hachette Book Group, Inc. First published in Great Britain in 2017 by Trapeze, an imprint of the Orion Publishing Group Ltd. Reproduced with permission of the Orion Publishing Group through PLSclear.

'A Flutter of Fairies' © Clare Bevan 2004. Reproduced by permission of the author.

'The Furies' © Lavinia Singer. First published in *Falling Out of the Sky: Poems about Myths and Monsters* (The Emma Press, 2015). Reproduced by permission of the author.

'The Dragon and the Undying' and 'Dryads' © Siegfried Sassoon by kind permission of the Estate of George Sassoon.

'Medusa and Minotaur Take Tea' © Rachel Piercey. First published in *Falling Out of the Sky: Poems about Myths and Monsters* (The Emma Press, 2015). Reproduced by permission of the author.